I Am a
DOLPHIN

Level 1

Written by Lori C. Froeb

Silver Dolphin

PRE-LEVEL 1: ASPIRING READERS

 LEVEL 1: EARLY READERS

- Basic factual texts with familiar themes and content
- Concepts in text are reinforced by photos
- Includes glossary to reinforce reading comprehension
- Phonic regularity
- Simple sentence structure and repeated sentence patterns
- Easy vocabulary familiar to kindergarteners and first graders

 LEVEL 2: DEVELOPING READERS

 LEVEL 3: ENGAGED READERS

 LEVEL 4: FLUENT READERS

Silver Dolphin Books
An imprint of Printers Row Publishing Group
A division of Readerlink Distribution Services, LLC
10350 Barnes Canyon Road, Suite 100, San Diego, CA 92121
www.silverdolphinbooks.com

ISBN: 978-1-64517-226-0
Manufactured, printed, and assembled in Shaoguan, China.
First printing, March 2020. SL/03/20
24 23 22 21 20 1 2 3 4 5

Hello! I am a dolphin.
Welcome to my ocean home.
My friends are waiting for me.

Come on! You can meet them.

I live in a group of dolphins called a **pod**.

The pod plays, hunts, and swims together.

We talk to each other with clicks and whistles.

We each have our own whistle.

My whistle is how others know me.

It is like having a name.

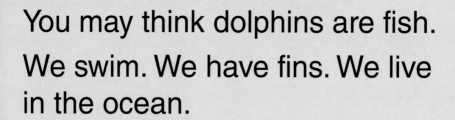

You may think dolphins are fish. We swim. We have fins. We live in the ocean.

But we are not fish.

We are **mammals** just like you.

We are **warm-blooded**. We breathe air.

We drink milk from our mothers when we are babies.

Dolphins are related to whales and porpoises.

humpback whale

beluga whale

porpoise

We are also related to hippos.
It is true!
The hippo is our closest
living **relative**.

I am a bottlenose dolphin.
My body is all gray.

I live in the warmer parts of the ocean.

There are thirty-eight other **species** of dolphin.

Most live in the ocean.

Some live in rivers.

Atlantic spotted dolphin

dusky dolphin

short-beaked common dolphin

spinner dolphin

Not all dolphins are gray.

Amazon river dolphins are pink!

They have long thin snouts.

Orcas are called killer whales.

But orcas are not whales.

Orcas are dolphins!

They are the largest dolphins in the world.

Do you see the hole in my head?

That is my blowhole.

All dolphins have one.

I must come to the water's surface to breathe.

I breathe through my blowhole.

I can also use it to make sound.

I use my blowhole to make my whistle and clicks!

I am getting hungry.
My pod is ready to hunt for food.

Big dolphins like orcas hunt for seals.

Some orcas even hunt sharks.

Bottlenose dolphins like to eat small fish and squid.

I hear some fish nearby.

I use sound waves to look for prey.

This is called **echolocation**.

I send a sound into the water.
The sound bounces off objects and back to me.

The sound tells me about the objects.
There is a school of fish nearby!

Dolphin pods hunt fish together.
They herd the fish into a large ball.

Then each dolphin swims through the ball.

We catch fish as we swim through.

Some dolphins hunt another way.
They make a ring of mud in
the water.

The fish jump out of the water to
escape the mud.

The dolphins catch jumping fish!

Dolphins do not chew their food.

Our teeth are only good for grabbing.

We swallow our food whole.

After lunch, it is time to play.

We love to play!

It is fun to flip out of the water.

We also like to surf the waves.

Sometimes we play catch.

We use things like seaweed, sponges, or coral.

Some of us make bubble rings for fun.

Jumping out of the water is fun.

Swimming in water takes a lot of energy.

Moving through air is much easier.

This is why dolphins jump out of water while swimming.

It is called **porpoising**.

Dolphins are curious and smart.
Some of us like to be around humans.
We sometimes play and swim together with humans.

Some dolphins have saved humans from drowning.

Some dolphins work with humans.

The dolphins are trained to look for lost swimmers.

The dolphins are rewarded with fish.

I hope you liked meeting my pod.
We are going to look for some waves.

It is time to play!

Glossary

echolocation: a method dolphins use to find objects using sound waves

mammals: animals that are warm-blooded and feed milk to their babies

pod: a group of dolphins, porpoises, or whales

porpoising: to jump out of the water while swimming

relative: animals or plants connected by common family members

species: a group of living things different from all other groups

warm-blooded: animals that control their own body temperature